Dew Drops

Relishing the Moment

By

Christi Ortiz

Cover Illustrated by:

Therese Schmidt

In gratitude:

For the gift

each moment brings,

that we may all

be open

to the encounter,

and learn to relish

the treasures within her.

For the gift

of so many great

teachers from many

faith traditions

that call us to awareness,

that call us to meet each moment

with open hearts

and open minds.

For Patricia Trautman,

mother and grandmother,

who inspired this book through

her passion for life,

her compassionate heart,

her love of prayer,

and Joy in living.

Her Spirit lives on

in the Love she poured out,

the Faith she lived out,

the contagious laughter she spread,

and the hunger she fed.

Thank you for the wisdom you shared

and for the reminder to *relish*

that which is important.

Welcome to the second book of this series, and a whole new set of poems for reflection!

If you are new to these prayer books, the introduction is included here for your reference. May you be abundantly blessed by the time you devote to these periods of reflection & contemplation.

Introduction

~~

Daily prayer is as essential as our daily meals for nourishment on the spiritual journey. However, so many of us struggle with quieting our busy minds and bodies enough to be able to taste and enjoy the stillness and the refreshment that prayer has to offer. This book is intended to be a doorway for prayer. Its poems and stories are intended to invite you into contemplation. It gives the reader a palpable focusing point to enter into a deeper communion and prayer, so that with the guidance of the Holy Spirit, the seeker may leave the images and words of the page only to be led to their own journey into the Divine and rest there. Readers are encouraged not to be limited by these promptings, but to only use them as their own springboards for reflection, meditation, and discovery. Further, this is not intended to be a book for entertainment, to merely glance at, or admire from afar. This is above all, an invitation, an invitation to go deeper, to let go, and surrender to the gift of prayer that is offered to all who will allow themselves to be taken up in her embrace.

How to begin

Although not essential, we encourage you to find a space for your prayer time. A place that is conducive to quiet, reflection, peace, and beauty. Our external environment has a great impact upon our internal state: including emotions, physical sensations, and stress perception levels. Thus, try choosing a space that is free of disruptions. We say "disruptions" to signify those things that would be a jarring interference or impediment to entering into a relaxed, meditative state. We do not say "distractions" because in actuality, things in the environment around you may be aides to your prayer experience. For example, nature can be a great catalyst for being immersed in a mystery greater than yourself and can be a very peaceful and grounding experience for many. Additionally, a special place, cushion, chair, or area set aside for meditation can be conducive for creating a sense of peace, calm, comfort and familiarity that can serve as an external cue for transitioning the body and mind to a state of quiet, reflection, awareness, relaxation, and harmony.

This space can be open; a place of beauty, in nature, by a window, decorated by art, a candle, plants, etc. Or it can be a small, closed, simple, private place (Mathew 6:6 and the idea of a prayer closet). Just choose what you are drawn to, where you are comfortable, what is convenient, and works for you.

We also suggest using a posture that works for you. Choose a position that will be comfortable and won't lead to pain and discomfort and require frequent posture changes. This can be sitting, walking, lying down, whatever is most conducive to attention, awareness, relaxation, and peace.

Additionally, it is helpful to choose a time of day that is right for you. This may be a time when you are alert and refreshed first thing in the morning. Or it may be when you are stressed and uncomfortable and need to seek solace and centering. It may be at the end of the day when you are relaxed and reflective of what has transpired and want space and a means to recollect. Try different times and see what works for you. The only caution we advise against would be to not try and squeeze this into a 10 minute break when you will be rushed and have a hard time focusing or entering into silence and contemplation. Give yourself the needed space and time before you have another activity you need to do so that you will feel the freedom to enter into the depths of your experience of the Divine.

How to use this book

Further, it is important to not see this book as a book to read. It is above all a prayer book; a book for reflection and meditation. It is not intended to be consumed in large amounts at one time! We encourage you to read slowly, one page at a time. If a certain word or phrase draws you, let the rest go and stay with that. Some words or phrases may seem rich with meaning or depth for you, like a sponge soaked with water, take the time to let the capacity of each word or image empty itself into you and above all, let the Spirit be your guide. Allow your thoughts and reflections ruminate with you throughout the day. Chew them slowly. Absorb what they have to offer. Interact with them, play with them, write your own. This is not intended to be a stale, one-way encounter; but a dance, an interaction. You will bring your life experiences, your world-view and belief systems. You will bring your memories and concepts, your values and preferences, your dreams, hopes, and longings. All of this will be part of your experience as well. Welcome these into the reading, let them interact with the words and images on the page. Allow the book to read you, to open you up to discover more about yourself past, present, and future. Uncover your inner wisdom. Let this touch an inner knowing within you and allow it to gurgle up into its own words, images, and stories. There will be times when you feel refreshed and enjoy the experience. It can be liberating and eye-opening, it can affirm what you always knew to be true for you. It can also challenge you or perturb you. You may be repelled by some things and attracted to others. Notice this. Sit with it. Let it speak to you about yourself and your experience. You can disagree with concepts and form your own ideas. You can feel drawn to write your own poems or create your own pictures and images. Let this book move you to your own Encounter with the Sacred.

Blessings on the Journey!
Christi Ortiz &Therese Schmidt

Table of Contents

Dew drops

I woke up one morning
completely dumfounded with dew.
It utterly fascinated me.
Surely I had seen dew before, or had I?

With its inconspicuous defiance of gravity
silently hanging from branches all around,
Innumerable drops of water
Still
Waiting
Motionless
Poignant

Full of potential
as if holding all the mysteries of the cosmos
in one tiny ball
shimmering droplets of perfection
everywhere.

I watched as they hung in there unchanging
until perhaps the rain began to fall
and another drop of water came
and the two coalesce into one
and the weight seems to be so great
that the droplet slowly releases
as if giving birth to itself
and falls to the puddle below

Yet, there remains the drop of dew as before
and if I reach out to touch it
it effortlessly releases itself
dissolving into wetness upon my hand.
Or when I press it to my lips
in an effort to taste its sweetness
I taste nothing

Like the manna in the desert,
the dew comes anew each morning: Gift
It cannot be stored, horded, captured, or clung to
only received, relished, enjoyed.
This manna sustained the Israelites
as they wandered in the barren desert
in search of the Promised Land
It nourished them anew each day
to continue the journey

The dew, so metaphoric of the tender fragility
of each present moment,
so easily trampled on and destroyed,
or not even noticed.
Pockets of grace
ready for the taking,
if we are but Aware.

Silence

Silence is the great act of faith
that if I sit here long enough,
You will come
and remove the veil.

If I were a mystic

If I were a mystic

I am sure that I would be

a painter, a musician, a dancer, and a poet

Though previously I never could

I would then

Though I have no skill for these arts

my soul would be compelled to spill over

to create the music inside

For when the soul is on fire with God

it must sing

Poor, Precious Beggar

I come to this world as a poor, precious beggar

with nothing to offer

Yet this does not lead me to grasping, hoarding,

or stealing in fear and lack

but rather gratitude for all received

and all that is naught.

What is the self?

What if this self I cling to
is like a big, heavy winter coat.
I have worn it so long
that I came to identify with it
saying, "this is who I am"?
But what if I try hanging it up for just a while,
suspend it just for a moment?
I can always put it back on again
if panic arises from the exposure.

Might a new reality and freedom open up to me?
I am not my coat!
I am free!
And perhaps another layer will come off,
and another.
Each time with a wonder in the awareness,
this is not me!
And when all the layers are stripped away
what will I be?

Life Underground

Life is like an underground subway
going round and round
like a merry-go-round.
All the passengers completely unaware
that they are on this ride
thinking this is all there is.
They fight over who gets the best seat,
the seat of honor.
They fight over who owns the one suitcase
in the luggage rack.

One day I decided to step off.
I walked up the stairs
and went outside.

For the first time I saw

a beautiful, wide world above

Holy and lovely.

I could scarcely believe my eyes.

How had I lived underground my whole life

like an ostrich with my head in the sand?

I was completely unaware.

Oh, the dread I had in having to go back down

and step onto that subway again

like a person coming back to their heavy body

after a near-death experience.

Yet this time I was determined

not to forget.

Wild Dance of Fury

I sit silently in a cozy, dark room.
A single candle flame my only light.
As I let the stillness sink into my bones,
I relish the silence
as the rest of the world seems to fade away.
In the calm the candle waves for my attention.
My awareness shifts to the single, flickering flame.
Why do you move about with such fury I ask?
Why not burn in stillness I wonder?
But the flame seems to taunt me,
like an energetic little child
inviting me to come and play.
Dancing around in wild swirls and dips
like the Dance of Shiva,
like the tongues of fire
coming to rest upon the Apostles,
like a Rabbi offering prayers at the Wailing Wall,
Or a monk engaging in thousands of prostrations
one after another in all directions.
This lone wick in a sea of melted wax
too filled with a dynamic force to stand still.
Dancing with vibrant life in one great display
as if to give its all before it is quickly snuffed out.
I wonder why I don't live this way.
This courageous candle teaches me a lesson.
It beckons me to live a life on fire with grace
living each moment in a wild dance of fury,
as if living out a sacred contract
to live each moment to the fullest,
never knowing when it will be the last.

Divine Embrace

The Divine cleaves to me

and won't let me go.

I am caught in Her fierce embrace

of awe, beauty, wonder, transcendence, and love.

No matter how I wiggle I can't shake this hold

that has captivated me.

She has paralyzed me in Her embrace

and won't release me until she has

poured her Sacred Mysteries into my soul.

I am seized in this web of Sacred.

Everywhere I turn, there She is

in a thousand forms and directions.

I cannot escape Her,

I am Hers.

Tears, our Holy Water

The world needs us to cry more,

to cry tears of repentance,

tears of grief,

tears of compassion,

tears of joy,

tears of relief,

tears of love,

tears of surprise,

cleansing tears,

tears of understanding,

tears of awakening.

Our parched land needs our tears

to soak in the thirsty ground.

How much evil would have been spared

if we had only shed more tears

and laughed more?

The two are so intertwined,

perhaps that's why one often leads to the other,

laughing to tears

and crying so hard until you laugh.

They are a release, a surrender.

Emotions are energy in motion,

they need expression.

Oh how we need our tears.

Some fear they have lost them for good

that they are buried so deep

only an earthquake would unearth them.

But they will come if we let them.

We must stop damming them up

in ourselves and others.

Such harm this creates.

A sad day it was when the first person

told the lie that you should not cry.

We need our tears.

We cannot lose touch with this holy watershed

and their power to cleanse and heal and unite

and clear the way for peace to sweep in.

Wu-Wei

Ancient wisdom reminds us

it is not in the doing,

the best things in life you cannot force,

like love, joy, peace, generosity,

forgiveness, and lasting change.

This is hard for our driven minds to understand

we're used to bulldozing our way through life

to get what we want,

our egocentric work ethic tells us:

good things come to those who work for it.

Yet, nature's wisdom often laughs

at our constant effort

when she can sweep in to create or destroy

in an instant

or slowly create magnificent rock formations

one drip at a time

so simple and delicate and patient

in no hurry to prove anything,

just letting it unfold.

Yet do not doubt her power and strength

when it is needed.

Anyone swept under her crashing waves

knows to respect her.

Yet she feels no need to strut in pompous achievement

She'd rather unfold her beauty and her mystery

in the blossom of a flower.

As you ponder this way of being in nature,

perhaps you might feel invited

to enter into her flow.

When one takes the time to see

the wisdom of this path,

the whip naturally seems to fall to the wayside.

It no longer makes sense to continue berating

one's own nature,

for there are destinations for which

no amount of striving can get you.

We know this, but I think we are afraid,

because doing is all we know.

We have not tried on the art of being,

afraid it will leave us naked, powerless.

In fact, part of entering into the Tao,

entails a letting go.

We opt for control, even if it is an illusion.

And so the struggle will continue.

Perhaps pride and fear tell us this is the only way.

Yet glimpses of this truth

will inevitable peek through

like rays of sun that shine in,

when the cloud passes by.

It may come at a moment

least expected and unsought.

Peel away the selfishness and anger,

love and forgiveness are born.

Still the noise,

and a wellspring of intuition will speak to you.

Like an athlete in the zone, or a child playing
there is a doing, without doing.
We are seeing now that we cannot fight for peace

and that we need to respect our environment.
Disasters of our own doing can wake us up
to our need for balance and harmony and respect.
So as we contemplate the lilies of the field
Let us turn to the words of the *Tao Te Ching*:

"The Sage is occupied with the unspoken
and acts without effort.
Teaching without verbosity,
producing without possessing,
creating without regard to result,
claiming nothing,
the Sage has nothing to lose".

Praying in the Dirt

I find that at this point in my life
I don't want to just pray in a Church
I want to pray in the dirt
I want to pray, not with my hands folded
but with my fingers in the earth
in my garden, as I watch plants come to birth
I want to pray as I play with my children
as we blow bubbles in the air,
as they rise up, so does our prayer.
I want to pray as I make love to my spouse
as we offer and receive the sacrament
of our bodies and souls
I want to pray with a friend in sorrow
I want to pray with a stranger
I want to pray while I work
I want to sing a song of praise
I want my life to become a prayer to you
and let you give life to my prayer.

Hide and Seek

A man came to me in distress
angrily exclaiming,
"You think God exists?
Show me, where was God when my wife died?
Where is God when children are abused,
Where is God in war and famine?
Where is God? Asleep? Dead? Hiding?"

"Yes, these are great evils"
I paused in silence for a long while.
Seeing I was making no excuses,
the man's anger passed and he sighed,
"Why does God not show Himself?"

And I asked him,
"If God were not hiding, would you seek Him?"

The Mystery of the Cross

If I were God,

I would have chosen a different way,

but perhaps only Divinity

could reach in to the depths

of man's folly to redeem it,

becoming human in every way,

reclaiming our divinity,

calling us Home.

Discovery

We are called to discover God as a little child. Have you ever watched a child just beginning to crawl and discover the world around them? They are full of energy and desire and curiosity. They vivaciously long to touch, grasp, smell, taste, and study each and every detail around them. There is nothing that surrounds them that hasn't been examined, held, pounded, and tasted. All of their energies are directed outward to uncover and explore their environment. Image if we took this same hunger to our prayer life with God. What if we sat with God with such curiosity and longing to discover, uncover, and explore the Divine Mysteries? What if we just spent time touching and tasting the Lord's presence? What joy the Lord would feel if we lunged forward with such longing and happiness at the beginning of our prayer encounter. Why do we make prayer so complicated, when in reality it is as simple as touch, when it can be as natural as our inner longing to connect, to discover?

Unlearning

Babies are natural contemplators; they contemplate the world around them. It is only through life that we unlearn how to pray and lose the ability to see things anew, to discover the world around us afresh like a tiny child. We often suffocate the ability to meditate out of our children and instill other values such as achievement and self-identification. Yet, in their natural state they have the ability to truly see the world around them. They are able to look at others without judgments, preconceptions, labels, or classifications; just true perception, naked seeing. In this openness and freedom they seem to possess an inherent wonder, curiosity, and enjoyment of the world around them, even the simplest of objects.

Take some time to contemplate your surroundings as if you were a small child. Perhaps you are seeing many of these things for the first time. You have not habituated to the various different colors, textures, shapes, sounds, and movements of the objects around you. Let yourself be curious, explore. Allow the objects to be absorbed into your consciousness through the five senses without needing to conceptualize, name, judge, or categorize them. Just experience them in raw form.

Next you can move to seeing, touching, smelling, tasting objects, places, or people in your imagination. Try seeing someone in your life as if for the first time. What do you notice? Try tasting a food as if for the first time, what textures, smells, tastes are aroused? What have you overlooked in your environment? Enter into these familiar places again, with a fresh outlook.

Ruach

I find it interesting
that most mediations
seem to start with awareness
of the breath
Perhaps this in and out of air
brings us to our primordial nature
as beings of breath.
For we know all so well
that minutes without this breath
means death.
It is the essence of life
This In and Out
Inhaling and Exhaling
Give and Take
there is an exchange that takes place
Oxygen coming in,
carbon dioxide going out
My breathing
changes the air around me
I participate in the Divine Breath
by receiving and inhaling
and letting go in exhaling
This return they call breath,
it is unique to all of us, yet universal
Breath
Both conscious and unconscious
it continues
Bidden or unbidden it is
Breath

Spirit

When this clay form dies and decays
and rejoins the earth from which it came
what happens to the Life Breath within me?
Surely it will go on being
Breath
Air
Spirit
Joining the Wind

The Space

I imagine I am a lump of formed clay
Hard and solid is my ego
Impenetrable my pride and selfishness
And then begins the skillful etching
of the Diamond Mind
Slowly, gently, effortlessly
the clay is carved away from within
A hollowness is created
Spaciousness is now
where hardness once was
Loving kindness, compassion, gentleness
sweep in to the newly formed space
Humility, respect, openness
have come to dwell here
in this clay pot of my body
I am now more the space that is
than the clay that was
With time the clay form will melt away
what will I be?

My Soul

My soul, a capacity for God

Like a cup made for Water

so my soul is made for you, oh God

Come and dwell in me

Pour yourself into me

I have made space for you

I offer you my hollowness.

God's Many Faces

I'm a wild, running horse.

I'm a meek, little lamb.

I'm a roaring lion,

and I'm a tiny mouse.

I'm a soaring eagle,

I'm a gentle kitten.

I'm a slow turtle,

and I'm a racing cheetah.

I'm a fluttering butterfly,

I'm a busy bee.

I'm a gnawing termite,

and I'm a building beaver.

I am not one, but all,

and nothing all the same.

Can you see my face?

Can you call my name?

I am hidden, and I am everywhere,

changing every day.

If you try and catch me and hold me,

you'll only be grasping thin air.

Instead, let me stay alive,

free and never known,

popping my head out,

at the changing of the seasons.

Don't judge by my looks.

Don't pretend to know me by my works.

But experience me anew,

like the blowing of the wind.

Leave me nameless,

and let me BE.

Once I was, then I wasn't,

but I still am today.

I'm ever changing; I never stay the same.

Yet there's a strand inside of me,

that always was and will be,

that is God.

Will you strain to see me as I am?

Don't hold on to the cocoon,

just because it is safe.

Let me break out and be created anew.

Do you have to hold on,

or will you let me fly?

Don't label, categorize,

& chart me away in the back;

I do not fit a mold.

You say you love me

because of who I was in the past.

But can you love me now,

and who I will be tomorrow?

Experience me anew each changing moment,

then you love me.

But will you let me be

so free?

Will you let me be born

and die again in a day?

Will you say hello and good-bye

in an instant?

I am not a dead sea,

or a still lake.

I am living, flowing water,

are you strong enough for the intake?

Who are you God?

I am the baby crying.
I am the old woman dying.
I am the stick that hits you.
I am the Faith that proves True.
I am the loved one's embrace.
I am the tear stained face.
I am the sunshine in the morn.
I am the rolling fields of corn.
I am the swaying trees.
I am the stinging bees.
I am the laughing heart.
I am the wounding dart.
I am the helping hand.
I am the spacious land.
I am the kind smile.
I am the bitter guile.
I am the Healer.
I am the Dealer.
I am the song of the bird.
I am the Living Word.
I am Faith, Hope, and Love.
I am the peaceful dove.
I am the long Fight.
I am the dark Night.
I am the breaking Dawn.
I am the gentle fawn.

I am the object of shun.
I am the Hidden One.
I am the king in a Palace.
I am blood flowing from the chalice.
I am the lonely, forgotten One.
I am the charity left undone.
I am Majesty and Splendor.
I am Redeemer and Mender.
I am Unwanted and Helpless.
I am poor and voiceless.
I am Victor and Humility.
I am Failure and Futility.
I am Patience and meekness.
I am Trust and Weakness.
I am Substance and Absence.
I am Mercy and Penance.
I am sin and death Destroyed.
I am life enjoyed.
I am suffering and sorrow.
I am yesterday and tomorrow.
I am the Resurrection and the Fall.
I am Nothing and I am All.
I am Love, I am God.
I Am.

Acceptance

Do you know what goes on

in the depths of my soul,

when I myself can't even seem to wade

through the muddy waters in my depths?

Oh yes, how glad I am that you know me better

than I know myself.

I do not need to list my wants, needs,

desires, and fears.

You know them all; you embrace them all.

Yes, you embrace all of me,

conscious and unconscious,

in understanding and acceptance,

asking only that I do the same.

Play in my Name

I didn't send you here to save the world.

I sent you here to play,

To drink deeply of the summer breeze,

to Laugh out loud,

and stop to notice the simple wonders

life has to offer.

Don't make things so hard, by forcing your way.

When you are living in the life flowing waters

of my Grace

You can just enjoy the ride.

Rest in me.

Surrender your hold on control.

Play in my Name.

Still Enough

Am I still enough to sink into your Depths,
to taste your Essence?

Do I have the Courage
to come Home to the Center?

Will I leave the periphery of life
to find its core?

Do I have the Discipline
to make the journey?

Oh Lord save me from surface dwelling,
and pull me into the darkness of your Heart.

Still the noise and confusion from above,
draw me into the Deep Caverns of your Love.

I let all the rest go,
to rest in Thee.

Bosom of God

Can you imagine how you would feel

nestled in the bosom of God,

Cradled in the awesome power

of the Alpha and Omega?

How could you fear or worry or doubt

surrounded by such love?

Silent strength holding you up

when you cannot stand.

Rest in the stream of God's peace

for She provides all.

You Are

The Delight of my Soul

The Hunger of my Being

My Beginning and my End

The Sustenance of my Life

My Strength and my Hope

The source of all Love

Comfort to the weary

Home above all homes

Peace amidst the storm

Healing to the nations

Salvation that makes us whole

Light in our darkness

Bearer of our burdens

Unity of our brokenness

Fountain of Grace

Molded and Melted

Created in your image and likeness?
Sometimes I find this so hard to believe,
when I look at myself.

I feel so alien, so separate
from you who
are Pure Love.

Yet, there is a voice inside that tells me,
if I stand here long enough,
in the rays of your piercing love,

If I lay myself bare before Your merciful gaze,
I too will come to be as you are,
the rest will melt away.

What is Truth?

The world tells you building up
your ego strength is the key
maximize your abilities, assets, and successes
to be all you can be,
work tirelessly to number them on your resume
and store them up for all to see.
This is the goal of life they tell me.

Yet, sometimes when I stop this frenzied rat race
long enough to sit and ponder,
I find myself questioning the wisdom of this path
and wonder:
Do we have it wrong?
Why must I compete with my neighbor
with such thunder?

And when I see a tsunami or earthquake
in an instant put it all asunder
I realize we are not the Gods that we preponder.
So if we have it backwards,
what then is this life all about?

Then I see a vision in the sky:
what appears to be tiny cells
too numerous to count
rising up, they are embraced by a great Expanse,
immersed in a brilliant Light throughout.
In awe of this great Power, Beauty, and Love
I had a knowing:
this was God without a doubt.
And the tiny beings' only separation
from total Union:
a membrane measured by Ego amount.

Awareness

The sunrise arouses me from my deep sleep
as the sunlight pierces through
my bedside window.
I peer out at the bursts of color
that dart across the sky,
and its beauty stirs me to wakefulness,
as if coaxing me to get out of bed ,
like an excited toddler
that can't wait to start the day.

I sit in quiet contemplation
for my morning time of praise
and as the flames of color begin to fade away
as quickly as they arose,
I begin to reflect on the gift each moment brings
and how we must be awake to the present graces
for if we are too busy to notice,
they quickly pass away.

So as I offer you this prayer time
in silent reflection
You offer yourself to me in return
and reveal that you are not only present
in the here and now.
You are the Eternal, the Always.
And call me to the awareness of this Truth.

You challenge me to the Divine game
of Hide & Seek.
You challenge me to find you hidden
in the events of my day.
You challenge me to recall this Awareness
as I scurry from place to place.
When the storms of emotions or challenges buffet
at my peace of soul
You remind me to seek refuge in You.
When I feel weary at the tasks ahead
I can find consolation in your Strength within me.

And at evening,
when I peruse back through the day
I am surprised to find you hiding
in the most unexpected places,
when I had no idea you were there.
You seem to giggle with delight at my recollection
& in your Divine Sense of Humor
you laugh & tell me,
"You may call it the Examination of Conscience",
but that's why I call it,
'the Examination of Consciousness'".

Lord of all Surprises

You are the Lord of all surprises.

You never cease to amaze me.

Continually you burst out

of the box

I put you in.

Like a Harp

You play my soul like a harp.

Every part is known to you.

You alone know my inmost being.

How I love to rest in your Presence.

I am made for you.

You alone complete me and make me whole.

For you my inner most being longs,

for reunion with its Maker.

Oh, Lord, thank you for how you love me.

Wholly and completely I am known and loved.

Nothing is hidden from you.

I am yours.

Theology

How can we study God?

How can we begin to grasp the great Theos?

We cannot resist the magnetism of our Creator.

Yet how can we come to know the Origin of all?

It is like trying to explore the Universe,

one may never grasp the immensity

of the vast expanse.

Yet the yearning pulls us onward.

Our hope sustains us in the journey.

Our faith, like the embrace of the sunshine,

warms the soul and reassures the seeker

that although God we will never fully know,

we have *always* been fully known.

Holy Ground

Sometimes life happens about us so fast that we don't stop to contemplate the sacred moments of our daily lives. We fail to recognize that countless encounters throughout the day are dripping of the Divine presence. We forget that our relationships, our homes, our work is holy ground. God is present, are we? Come to the awareness and notice the change in yourself and how you relate to the world around you, your very self, and the people you meet in your day. You may tread more lightly in your relationships. You may treat others with more tenderness and forgiveness. A respect and gratitude may wash over you, as you realize, truly, you are on Holy Ground.

Hearer of the Word

Why oh Lord am I here?

Why have you created me?

What is the purpose of my life?

Why must I endure this suffering?

When will you call me home to yourself?

Oh, my child you *are* home,

The kingdom of God is at hand.

I am Love,

and I created you out of Love,

for Love must have a recipient.

Love must be freely given and freely received.

Your life is a Divine Gift.

Receive it.

My love has been freely given.

Receive it.

When you receive me into yourself,

the boundaries of your ego burst open,

you dissolve into my Presence,

and become One with me,

I live in you and you in me.

This is what it means to be,

a Hearer of the Word of God,

to receive the Word made flesh,

to taste and see the goodness of the Lord,

to celebrate Life!

To celebrate the Eucharist,

the Great Thanksgiving,

where you become what you receive.

Gratitude, the response,

to the gift of Life!

Transforming Gaze
Based on 2 Cor 3: 17-18

As I gaze at you
I open myself to you
to gaze into my soul.
I lay myself bare, like an empty bowl.

Peer into the deep recesses of my heart.
Plant your grace within me, never to depart.
Turn the darkness bright.
Make my face reflect your Light.

Transformed by the power of your glance
imparted by your Spirit: the freedom to dance.
Our lives tell the salvation story,
changed from glory to glory.

Mold me unto you,
make my love more true.
I am yours and you are mine
in this Covenant Divine.

Tasting Your Hidden Presence

What if I listened

Deeper

and

Longer

What would I hear?

How would I change?

What if what I know to be prayer

is not prayer at all

but just inner static?

What if I knew true stillness

and tasted your Presence?

Surely I would never be the same.

I would come here often

to be with You

and

Drink.

Spiritual Bifocals

I knew a woman who used to sing
"I was blind, but now I see"
In confusion, I asked her,
"how can you claim to have been blind,
you've always been able to see."

With a smile she responded,
"Ah yes, I could see the temporal world,
all my worries & concerns, my goals & anxieties,
I went about my days seeing what was before me,
but, I never saw what was beyond me."

"I saw my own small world,
but I was blind to all the rest."
"Like what?", I asked perplexed.
"Like my neighbor down the street in need,
like the beauty in the smallest things,
or the gift that each moment brings".

Incredulous I inquired,
"How did this transformation happen?"
"Well, quite unexpectedly, I must say,
I was giving God my morning speal
with my litany of requests, preoccupations,
my needs, and complaints,
when suddenly she interrupted my monologue".

A bit jarred, I sat up and listened,
(I wasn't accustomed to God talking back)
She gently cupped my face in her hands
and responded,
"My child, all these things, I know them".
She spoke with such love and tenderness
that instantly I was assured,
I trusted her Words and knew she cared for me
and did not need my reminders.

We sat in silence for some time
and a new peace seemed to crawl into me
and rest there.
There didn't seem to be as much need for words.
And then she took my hand and bid me to follow,
"I want to show you something new".

And that is when she began to open my eyes
to a reality that had always been present,
had always been with me,
but of which I had been unaware.
I saw events of my life in a whole new light.
People I had known my whole life
suddenly were new to me.

With this intrigue came a great sense of love
for all that I saw.
What was in front of me was no longer bare
with all its flaws and ineptitudes.
It was permeated with a wholeness
and a harmony.
The temporal was embraced and held
by the Eternal

In awe and gratitude I asked God
how this could be,
"How could I have gone so long
without ever seeing,
without ever being aware
of what was right before me?"
She smiled and responded,
"It's simple, you need bifocals to see".
"Bifocals? But I've never worn glasses,
I have perfect vision".

Then, with a raised eyebrow,
she laughed and replied,
"Yes you have always been able to see
what is before you,
but now I am calling you to see beyond,
to see with my lens."

I sat breathless for a while taking this in.
I hadn't bargained for all this
when I started my morning prayer.
I needed to get on with my day,
and here God is showing me that I have been blind
and didn't know it,
and now instead of curing me, gives me glasses!
Knowing that all this was a bit much for me,
God reassured me,
"it's quite easy to see, just turn to me"

"Come to me in prayer frequently
throughout the day,
to exchange a narrow vision,
for a deeper, larger perspective.
I will give you my vision
for whatever you are facing.
Yes, it might be easy to go back
to seeing the world in the old way,
but do not fear, with these Spiritual Bifocals
you will see as I see.

Theophany

How long I have searched for you
in ancient Churches and pious prayers,
in hours of solitude and silence,
in acts of service and sacrifice,
I have pursued you far and wide.
In anguish and in longing,
I have sought you in the deep,
only to find you naught.
And when, in exhaustion and despair,
I slumped down in disbelief,
out you came from nowhere
and yet, all at once, I was conscious
of you present everywhere.
You showed yourself veiled
in the Guise of the Eternal Now.
Each moment you reveal yourself in a new way,
like a firefly that illuminates the dark sky
for but a moment.
And I in my temporality want to grasp you
and hang on to you to hold you forever,
to carry you with me in security wherever I go,
but alas, you are the Ineffable One
and I cannot grasp you in my palm,
for in so doing, in my lust for possession,
I kill the fragile spark of Divine Life
pregnant in each passing moment

And so, when I stop my grasping
and breathe
a long, slow, deep, breath,
I taste you.
I feel you soak in my bones
and I know you are and always will be.
And I exhale in peace
and feel your presence surround me
and penetrate me through
like the intense warmth of a summer sunrise,
as I let go and watch you unfold before me.
Now in this knowing,, I realize this Presence
has always been with me.
But I, in my pursuing,
chased you away from my sight,
not perceiving your showings
inherent in every moment.
So now, from time to time,
I stop my hustle and just sit
and wait,
and soak,
And let your aroma envelop me
like a thousand lilacs in bloom
and I surrender,
You alone are God.

Sophia

How beautiful she is
when she lets her hair down
and dances among the peoples of the earth
when she leaves her footprints upon your soul

You must wait in patience
and listen silently
to hear the sacred drums beneath the earth
to which her rhythm beats

Her dance echoes throughout the world
beckoning to her lost children
to come home to her bosom
and drink of her sacred milk

Her ancient lullaby
calms the anxious soul
as her sweet song
imparts her wisdom to the simple

Sweet Sophia
how you whisper to me
upon the winds of grace
and leave your kiss upon my face.

Living and Abiding

Oh, living and abiding Word of God,
Come to dwell in me.

You are a faithful God.
Once you speak into being,
Your presence never leaves.

You never cease pouring yourself into creation,
in ever new and abounding ways.

When I stop to breathe in the wonder of it all,
I am touched by the beauty & the sanctity of life.

Your Divine Life pulsates through the veins of
creation, giving it life in abundance.

Oh, living and abiding Word of God
thank you for the gift of Yourself
to dwell within us.

Cast out into the Deep

Like a clear, blue spring you call my name.

I notice you glistening from afar,

beckoning me to come,

inviting me to your refreshing waters

down below,

promising to quench my thirst

with your Heavenly Abundance,

and soothe my aching body

with the stillness of your caress.

My yearning to be immersed in you

increases as I approach.

The sweetness of the sanctuary you offer

is palpable

and your Smell fills the air around me

with the mist of your Presence.

There are other distractions

that bid for my attention

but nothing can squelch the hunger

beginning to gurgle within me.

You draw me to something deeper

than I have ever known,

yet somehow familiar, as if from my origins.

There is a sense that this is where I belong,

that this is what I am called to.

And so I dare to go further, closer, to enter in.

At first I dabble & splash just to get my feet wet

to examine what you are about

But you are not satisfied with purely rational,

philosophical analysis.

You want my whole self.

Breath of God

Breathe on me.

Your Spirit makes all things new.

the Power of your Life Breath

lives within me,

renews me daily.

Live in me.

Carve out new space in me

for your Holy Presence.

Teach me to Trust in You.

Enlighten me to See You.

Live in me,

Oh Breath of God.

Emptying

Oh you of little Faith and great Fear,

What will it take for you to surrender?

To let go of your great Fear?

You cling to It, though it serves you not.

Your heart blocked from receiving

the blessings which are yours.

Your hands are full.

You must come to me empty,

with Trust, Surrender, Faith.

Behold, I stand at the door and knock.

Will you open your heart to me?

Can you trust me with yourself?

I will wait.

I will wait for you.

I will wait for you to Trust Me,

so that I may come to dine with you,

and you may receive of my abundant Self.

Peace

May your kingdom come.

May your peace reign in our hearts.

The peace that comes from knowing,

knowing that you are enough.

The peace that comes from trust,

from trusting in your promises and faithfulness.

The peace that comes from letting go,

surrendering, sharing, grieving, letting go.

The peace the comes from forgiveness,

forgiving our enemies, our friends, ourselves.

The peace that comes from healing,

a deep healing inside and out.

The peace that comes not from external calm

but from an internal strength, a gift given to all

who will receive the Wisdom you teach.

Peace

Taste and See the Goodness of the Lord

As a deer longs for flowing streams,

so my soul longs for you, Oh God.

Why do you long oh my soul?

Do you not see me in early morning dew,

or feel me in the air within your chest,

or perceive me in the smile of a child,

or in the caress of a loved one?

I am nearer to you than you are to yourself.

Come drink of my Presence,

Come quench your thirst in me.

For as much as you thirst for me,

I thirst for you even more.

Womb of God

Spark of life

Creative energy

Born of love

In the womb of God

We live and move,

and have our being.

Embraced in Light,

Nourished and caressed,

in this sacred space.

One thing alone is necessary,

to be still

and know

that you Alone

are God.

Window of my Soul

Like crumbled pieces of glass,
we offer our broken lives to God.
We surrender the twists and turns,
the falls, the pits, the messes
as well as the joys, the gifts, the beauty.
He sweeps them all up like precious treasures
careful not to leave out a single sliver.
He blesses them all with the Kiss of His Breath
and as His Spirit pours over the jumbled pile.
They are brought together in wholeness.
With the glue of Mercy, the broken pieces
are made whole, holy.
Each piece is honored for its contribution
and when surrendered to the Hand of God,
begins to become a part of the pattern
of the One who Sees and Knows All.
The stained glass masterpiece is made from
the Master who pieces it together
And as He shines His Light through it,
it takes on an eternal dimension.
As each element becomes aglow with Love.
it radiates and sparkles with the Divine Light
Every piece finds peace, afire with God,
finally Home.

Dancing in the Rain

Darkness covers her mantle over the sky
Rain beats down upon the earth
Coolness sweeps in
as you, Oh God, let your long hair fall down
and gently sway and caress the earth
As you twirl in a dance of love with your creation
You embrace her and draw us near
Cherishing our presence
like every good mother you love us
and let us be free to be and create in your image

But sometimes this world seems
so empty of your Presence
dark and dreary with suffering
at every corner and on every face
So many calling out, "where are you God?"
But I know your Heart holds
and feels all this pain too
And your heart is big enough
to hold all the suffering of this world
and still have Hope
and still house Love
and still go on
dancing in the rain

Spark of Divinity

The spark of Divinity within us

can never be separated

from its cradle of humanity.

It is precisely in our sickness and frailty

where we encounter your Life within us.

The mystery of incarnation

will continue to baffle the mystics

yet its reality

so tangible

it is impossible to deny.

To Dust You Shall Return

Lists of worries tumbling around in my head
Problems I can't solve bringing fear and dread
This is my dismal state of insomnia, lying in bed

Then suddenly, a peace befalls me
A warmth passes over my body, leaving it free
As it travels it releases tension as all anxieties flee

A profound sense of being held
Coddled in love's embrace, my joy swelled
as all fears were quelled

Surrounded by such love and care
Why would I choose such burdens to bear
When freedom is found in the simplest prayer

Bathed in this light so bright

Those heavy concerns now seem so light

giving an assurance, "everything will be all right"

All my needs will be provided for

In this embrace, I long for nothing more

This is all that is needed at the core

The rest will pass away

As all things impermanent decay

Losing the veneer of significance

as they return to clay

Through this new gift of sight so strong

I see the true nature of these burdens

I've carried my lifelong

And, I let them fall to the dust at my feet,

where they belong.

The Divine Humility

How is it that God allows Herself

to be magnified in creation?

How is it that the Divine Lover

loves Her creation enough,

to stoop down to it and become one with it?

Oh, the humility of God!

Like a famous painter that lends Her canvas

to the clumsy brushstroke of a little child

out of Her love for the child

and what she might create.

She gives her freedom to become as she is.

She does not need the child's art,

yet She sees it as good and blesses it.

Oh, the humility of God!

And yet what beauty bursts forth

from this Divine Generosity

God and Her Creation intermingled

as paints on a canvas

The colors dance together

to become something beautiful

Limitless are the possibilities

when God pours Herself out

into creation without holding back

anything of Herself.

Earthen Vessels

The more we yield and submit
to the Potter's Gentle Hand,
the more we don't become hardened, hidden,
and afraid in our earthennes,
but instead humble, malleable clay in your Hands,

For we hold this treasure in earthen vessels,
you made us from the dust
and don't expect us to be any more than dust,
but only ask us to be open to receive
your Life giving breath into our being,
to receive your Spirit into the earthen clay
of our hearts and lives.
May the water of Your Mercy
soften the hardness of our hearts,
and mold the clay of our beings
into Your image and likeness.

If we submit, You will do the building,
the shaping, forming, and transforming.
If we come, you will build us,
you will use us to build the Kin-dom of God,
not because you need us,
but because you choose us, want us,
because You love us

You never fail or forsake your Creation.
We are not the sum of our weaknesses and failures
but the sum of the Father's love for us
and of His ability to transform us
into the image of His Son,
when we receive and say Yes
to Your Sanctifying Spirit with in us,
when we give the soil of our lives
over to you in humility,
to be broken and built into what You Will.

Your Will be done Lord Jesus,
Your Kingdom Come,
And may I be open to Your coming
in me, with me, through me,
Not later, not when I am perfect, but now,
in the Eternal Now
You are Present,
a Present held with human hands,
A Host in an Imperfect Hostess,
A Divine gift in a Human vessel,
A Divine mission in an earthy boat,
on the waters of this world,
but blown by the
Spirit of God.

Nameless One

Though you are more intimate to me
than I am to myself
and you have numbered every hair on my head
I can't begin to grasp who you are

.

Like fog, the more I try and grab you
and claim you as my own
the more you escape me
You are the Ineffable, the Nameless One

If I try and put you in a box,
You jump out.
If I limit you with my concepts
You break every molded image

For my heart is too small
to contain your Great Love
And my mind is too small
to grasp your Great Knowledge

Yet I will not cease seeking you
whom my heart loves
Though I will never hold you
I am content to be held by you

For I am known by the Unknowable One
For your Hand touched me
in the stillness of the womb
and the ripples have radiated out ever since

My life a journey of receiving you
and giving you myself
Yet I know it will take all eternity
to know you

Meeting God for the First Time

Like an orphan
he wandered most his life,
empty and alone,
wishing he had never been born.

He was bounced around from place to place
in a cruel, dark world,
never feeling at home in the world,
or in his own being.

He was angry and confused,
loathing the world and himself.
He would yell out to
the God that didn't exist.

And God heard his prayer
and the sky opened up
and She smiled at him
and he saw God.

At once he was enveloped
in the Alpha and Omega.
And although Her Voice held ancient power
it was tender and sweet,

as she so intimately spoke to him,
"You are my beloved son
I have loved you with an everlasting love.
I have always been with you.

In fact, I was so close to you
that you didn't know I was there,
the hidden ground of your being
that silently nourishes your life".

And he saw for the first time,
the love that had always been there.
He heard for the first time
the Voice he knew to be God.

Reflections

Art is a participation in the Divine.
The soul's energy needs expression
to love, to laugh, to create.

Painting, dancing, sculpting, building
quilting, cooking, gardening,
singing, playing, writing,

all the soul's expression of Love
to God and to the world,
a gift to the Giver of All.

The artist listens to the call
"You did not choose me, but I chose you
to go and bear fruit that will last"

Creative expression is the soul's
response to God
for the gift of life and love.

The soul becomes restless
when it cannot find an outlet
for the wellspring within.

For at its birth, the soul
was given a kiss of the Divine
created in the image of the Creator,

and given a mission, a desire
to share in the Creative Resurrection
of the world.

Art becomes a window to our Creator,
for there are endless reflections
of the Divine Image.

Ministry

When that person knocks at my door,
searching, seeking, asking for my help,
I open with a sense of love and care,
answering a call I can't deny.
Yet, I feel a subtle awe
at the task we are to undertake,
like standing at the edge of the cliff
& feeling the crashing waves
beat against the rocks.
The power and the mystery of God
like the vast ocean,
how can we begin to grasp the Ineffable One
I feel so small and inept in the face
of such great Majesty.
I gasp, "Oh Lord, I am in over my head"
God chuckles back,
"How could you not be?
Do not be afraid, that's right were you should be."
And so we begin.
I know there is no way I can navigate
the powerful, deep, profound waters ahead.
So I quickly give the wheel to God.
I know no matter how much I learn and study,
no matter how many times I've done this before,
I am never qualified for the journey.
I am always a poor, lost beggar
searching for the Way.

Yet, I do not fear my own inabilities
because I trust the search,
I trust the seeker,
and above all I trust the One Sought.
And so we set sail together
into the vast waters of the Divine
in our humble, earthen vessels
trusting the gentle breeze of the Spirit.
In faith, we cast out into the deep
unsure what shores we might find
and like the one we've left behind,
we let the waves of grace flow upon us.
In the end there is no map, or rule, or guide
but the one that burns within the seekers Heart.
After all, I am not here to *direct*
but to sit with, and witness the journey.
There's beauty in that Presence
peace, in that stillness and willingness
to honor another's experience,
to give the prayer of accompaniment.
There's no agenda, no hurry.
After all, we're already in the Water.
It's not so much about where we are going
but learning to be where we are now.
And so we sit together
sometimes in silence
but always aware of the Presence
within and around us as we float.

The Interface

A wise, old sculptor once told me,

that one of her greatest joys in working with clay

is the tension that is created

between what she wants the clay to do

and in what the clay is actually doing.

And it made me wonder...

might this be how God feels in giving us free will?

Yes, it has caused such destruction and evil,

but it has also given birth

to such Beauty, Love, and Truth.

Perhaps free will was one of God's

greatest acts of creativity.

Perhaps in the freedom to choose,

true Love is born.

Perhaps grace is found precisely in the Interface,

between God's will and our own.

Who can know God?

A man came up to me and asked,
"Do you know the Lord?"

I chuckled and replied,
"Who can know God?"

"But you have given your life to God?" he exclaimed.
"Yes!" I replied.

"And you spend your days serving God?"
"Yes"

"And you spend hours in prayer?"
"Yes"

"Then, how can you explain this?"
"I am drinking from a bottomless well"

Domus Dei et Porta Coeli
(House of God, Door to Heaven)

What if we were *aware*,

that we *are* a Temple of the Holy Spirit,

the Body of Christ, the House of God?

What if we lived our lives as if

it were a doorway to Heaven?

What if we perceived your Face

in each moment of grace?

How small our problems might seem,

in the shadow of your infinite Horizon.

Our weaknesses and doubts would crumble,

in the vast ocean of your Divinity.

Everything would be the same,

yet different.

Changed by the knowing

of the Sacrament of each present moment

I AM

I cried out, I cried out to the Lord

"Come to me, come to me"

And God responded,

"Come to me, I AM already here"

The Burning Bush

I wonder what caught Moses' attention
in the burning bush
Surely he had seen many fires in the desert
While out tending his flock
Why was this fire any different?
This fire that seemed to be contagious
And engulf him in its flame
Never to be the same
Propelled on a journey
Back to Egypt
To his homeland
To free his people
And in doing so, himself

The burning bush was unique
in that it was on fire but not burned up
Consumed by God, yet not destroyed
And from the luminescent energy comes
The profound truth of the words,

"I am that I am"
the understanding that God is beyond
all names and concepts and labels
this encounter begins Moses' life-long contemplative
journey
of beholding the face of God
which later transforms his own face
to glow with the Light of God
he himself becomes the burning bush

He beckons us to follow him out of bondage
He calls us to the freedom of love
He call us to be aflame with God
And to encounter God in our lives so that
We see every bush ignited with the fire of God
Every person aflame with the Spirit of God
And we take off our shoes
For we realize we are on
Holy Ground

Spiritual Discovery

What if I had the courage to break open my pursed
lips and share my dreams with you?
What if I let my heart go wild and tell you who I am,
where I've been & what I see on the horizon?
What if I let go of the fears and preoccupations
and reached deep into my soul to draw forth my
deepest longings? What if I had the courage
to put them into words, or song, or dance?
And in doing so, what if they became more a part of
my life and I began to play with them like a little
child and enjoy them, and get comfortable with
them? What if I no longer buried them for fear of
failure, scoffing, hard work, change, or doubt?
Maybe Faith is something that grows like yeast the
more you use it and put it into action.
Lord, give me the Faith to let your dreams come
alive in me. Enable me to wait in stillness with you
in the inner most chamber of my soul
to allow you to whisper my dream to me.
And when I leave the silence to go about my day,
permit me not to forget your words, your vision, my
dream. And most of all, allow me not to hoard it or
hide it away, but begin to share it, and thus live it.

May my heart be wide

I pray that I am supple and ready
that my heart is as soft
as the powdery soil of spring
That my mind is as open
as the wide eyes of a toddler
gleefully greeting each passing moment
as the wonder that it truly is
I pray my tears have the courage
to flow freely
and make music
where sorrow dwells
I pray my heart is wide
welcoming all who enter her gates
with love
I pray my mind is open
ready to sail the vast seas
of knowledge that lay before it
I pray my tears have compassion
to cry with those who suffer
and not grow weary
I pray my heart is wide
I pray my heart is soft
I pray my heart is wide

I Bow

Normally I bow in respect to others

I bow to their virtues that shine out

like stars in the dark night

But tonight I am compelled to bow to myself

and honor my own courage and strength

I bow to the struggles I have endured

I bow to the love I have chosen

I bow to the patience I have offered

and the generosity I have shared

I bow to the sacrifices and the strength

and maybe,

maybe, if I did this more

this part of me would grow

until I become

what I truly am:

Goodness

Compassion

People ask me how I think so well of others
how I can treat them with such
compassion and gentleness
giving them the benefit of the doubt,
and seeing their positive qualities.
I tell them that this is not
a Polly Anna, naïve approach
that ignores the faults and failings,
the weaknesses and wrongdoings
It does not ignore the scars and battle wounds
that have taken their course upon the person's life
But I tell them the reason I can look
with eyes of love,
the reason I can see goodness
where hate, revenge, and anger abound
where pain and suffering abide.
I tell them it is because everyone I've ever met
has turned out,
to be human.

The Lie

A world of lonely, hungry, abandoned orphans
hungry for love, hungry for belonging,
hungry for validation.
Empty, alone, wandering lost,
trying to find themselves
trying to find love
only to come up empty handed.
Crying children bumping into one another
begging the other to love them
pointing fingers
blaming, hating, hiding, lonely, unloved.

We wonder why we have wars.
We wonder why we have prejudice,
discrimination, and oppression.
Is that the truth?
Is that the life we were meant to live?
I don't believe so.
I believe somewhere, somehow a lie
was planted in the seed of humanity.

A lie that said "you are not loved",
"you need the approval and acceptance of others
to know your own true worth".
But I say that's a lie.
I say your dignity
is as essential to your being
as your very being itself
and can never be taken away in any way
through the actions of others or that of your own.
Your dignity, your value, your worth is yours
and it is only those who claim it
those who hold it like a flag of peace
waving the white banner high
that are able to love another
that are able to love this hungry, hurting world
that are able to bring peace
because they have first found it within themselves.

The Way

You may not be a mystic

or keep company with saints

You may not sit in meditation with the Buddha

or swap stories with Jesus and his friends

You may not take walks along the way

with Lao-tzu

Or join hands with Mohammad in prayer

But if the work you do is enlightening to you

If it illuminates your world

and makes those around you brilliant

Then follow your passion

whether the crowds follow you or not

You will have found your purpose for being

You will have found your reason for living

and peace in dying

Sentinels of Hope

We are called to be sentinels of hope
Seers of the unseen
Doers of the Word
Living by a power not from us
Loving from a Source inexhaustible
Believing in a reality unknown
Holding out for peace and healing
Standing up for justice and truth
Speaking up for the oppressed
Praying for those forgotten
Reaching out to the lonely and rejected
Hearing the voiceless
Breathing in gratitude for the blessings
Being at peace within ourselves and o

ur world
Persevering on the path
Throwing our hands up in praise
And our heads back in laughter
Greeting each new day as it comes
Grateful
To be sentinels of hope

The Beauty of Art

The world cries out for the artist.
It cries out to say,
"Make me beautiful.
Will you have the courage to look
in the face of suffering, death,
destruction and hopelessness
and still have the courage to paint,
to create music,
to build, to love, and to laugh?"

The world cries out for the artist
to be the one to say,
"We still have hope
There is beauty yet in her face
disfigured as she may be
broken and at war with herself".

The earth cries out to say,
"Paint me, make me beautiful
Love me still
Hope in me".

As long as we can still make art
humanity, the earth, life itself
can go on living with hope.
It is the art that brings us home to ourselves
And helps us to know ourselves again
when we have been lost by the fight of the world.

It is art that calls us home
and calls us beyond ourselves
to a vision of a new future
that is beyond our imagining
but somehow is created when
the paint brush meets the canvas
and the fingers touch the strings
when the dancer finds her rhythm
and the singer loses himself in the note,
that is when hope lives on,
that is when the world finds herself again,
when art becomes a beacon
of what is still possible.

The Question for the Quest

A man asks an itinerant hermit,

"who are you?"

And the wanderer replied,

"I forgot"

"What are you searching for?

Why have you left home, family, work?

For what?"

And the eremitic fool replies,

"I forgot"

You see, he no longer needed the journey

He had found himself and was already home

He no longer knew his name

because he no longer was

He was all places and people

This Moment

This moment offers

me eternity when I

stop to See and Be

Water Flow

Ice is made

Of intricate crystals

Beautiful webs

Of complex designs

Masterpieces of nature

Frozen in time

Water contains them all

But holds nothing

No grasping

No capturing

No control

No crystal

Just Flow

Just Letting Go

You only find life

You only find life
when you have died to your beliefs and ideals
You only have freedom
when you have suffered long enough
from your chains
You only become whole
when you have allowed yourself to be broken
You only embrace peace
when you have endured tension's friction
and found stillness
You only find acceptance of what is
when you have let go of what is not
and what you want to be
You only find now
when you have surrendered the past
and released the future
You only find yourself
when you have searched long and hard and then
forgot the search all together
This is when you are home
and when you have no home because you have left
on the wings of the dawn

Laughter, Soul Language

Laughter is one of life's greatest treasures

I try to drink it in deeply whenever I hear it

especially the laughter of children

Children's laughter hasn't been

tempered over the years

by social constraint or the weight of the world

that hinders one from perceiving

the hilarity of each moment

They can enter whole-heartedly

into their belly laughter

holding nothing back

releasing their delight

into the still air around them

I make it a point to relish my children's laughter

It comes often and easily

product of their joyful and carefree nature

Often I make their laughter my meditation

reminding me not to take myself

or life too seriously,

reminding me to stay present to the moment

As they throw their grand guffaws

without restraint

I am reminded of the Joy of humility & surrender

so enticing that you can hardly

restrain from joining in

I let the joyous sounds refresh my soul

and heal my weary body

as hope settles in the place

where the laughter stole my stress

It is here in these moments

that I know the veracity of Jesus' words,

"You must become like a little child

to enter the Kingdom of God"

The Plunge

The search for God

cannot be an escape

from the world

but rather plunge us into it

embracing the difficult, the joyous,

and the mundane,

God encompasses and imbues it all.

Mercy

I gave up on perfection
I traded it in for mercy

Mercy is a much better companion
She allows me to sleep at night

She treats me with gentleness and kindness
rather than harsh judgments and expectations

I have room to breathe
and love myself in my humanness

I can accept what is
without resistance or illusory attempts at control

I can trust in a power greater than myself,
the power of love to cover a multitude

I realized that I could only have one or the other
so I let go of perfection in order to embrace mercy

I have freed myself from the bonds of "should"
and now live in the blooming
that has grown in this new expanse

Stillness

Stillness is not the absence

of noise within,

but instead sailing above it

as calm as a boat in the ocean

as the waves are crashing nearby.

God's Presence

It's impossible to live outside of God

No matter what challenges I face this day

I do so, in God's Presence

Borrowed

Some think gratitude
is a difficult thing to cultivate

But it takes just a moment
of awareness

to glance around and see
that all I have

all I am
is borrowed

My body was built and borrowed
from my parents cells

The air I breathe
most likely someone else's air recycled

My clothes
were made by someone else

My food
grown and picked by someone else

My language
passed on & created by many others before me

The car I drive
designed and made by others far away

The house I sleep in
made by hands I know not

The fire that warms me
created and discovered long ago

My beliefs and ideas too
were given as a gift & passed down the centuries

My favorite song
created and shared by others

Virtually everything I see and touch and hear
is not mine

From this vantage point
Gratitude is the only response

God's Creativity

Only God could create
the unspeakable beauty of this earth
and then give us eyes to see it
Imagine if you had no vision?
Only God could inspire such divine music
and then give us ears to hear it
Imagine your life without melodies and laughter?
Only God could design the great variety
of scrumptious foods
and then give us the ability to taste it
Imagine never being able to taste?
Only God could contrive
the poignant array of aromas
and then give us a nose to relish their scent
Imagine your favorite smells.
Only God could invent the warmth of hugs,
fleecy softness, and tender kisses
and then give us skin to feel the world around us
Imagine never having the sensation of touch?
Only God could sneak in Her presence amidst the
world around us in a million silent ways
and then give us the intuition to perceive Her
Imagine those times you've been filled with Knowing

My prayer closet

The cocoon
that enables me
to break out

to break the shell
of ego
of fear and doubt

of self-centered thinking
of concepts and illusions
attachments and aversions

These false identities
slowly begin to crack
and lose their hold over me

With time, the cocoon
is no longer the safe
and comfortable cell it once was

Now I fly
The bonds are broken
I am free

I am

I become so enveloped by nature
that I sink into the depths of the earth,
and I become the dirt beneath my feet
and the grass that covers the prairie.

I am the ducks that play in the pond.
I am the breeze blowing by,
and the sky encompassing it all.
I am the clouds that are here for a moment
and then disappear.

Meditation

Meditation opens me up
to the spaciousness within me
and of which I am a part.

The Observer

I watch my life like a movie.

Sometimes I am moved to laughter

and sometimes I cry,

yet all the while knowing

that I am the observer

telling the story

as it passes by.

Impermanence

If we could only realize impermanence,

we would gain our freedom

from the ego's grasp.

Its hallow shell would reveal

that which has hatched

is already long passed.

Flowing River

Life is like a flowing river,

always passing by.

Joy comes along

and depression too,

self pity

and gratitude.

The key is not to jump in at any moment

assuming that this is so,

for if you but wait,

it too will pass on by,

giving space for the next.

We must learn not to identify with,

to embody

that which is impermanent,

but instead,

let it flow by.

Happiness

The awakened state that you truly are
buried underneath the rubble of
the ego's illusions and delusions.
Wipe off the dust
and you will see.

Congruence

Your meditation must flow

into your daily life

and your daily life

must flow into your meditation,

so that right action

becomes your first response.

Liberation is not an escape

from reality

but a descent into it.

Emptiness

Everything an illusion,

all things subsumed

in the Void.

Emptiness,

the only thing

that stays the same.

The ego, a delusion.

attachments, the chains.

Freedom, found in sight,

in letting go

into the Void.

Heartbeat of the Earth

As the heartbeat of the earth

pulsates through my veins,

I know that separateness,

is an illusion.

Religion is like a recipe

Religion is like a recipe

that points the Way

to the Tao, the Dharma,

the Way, the Truth, and the Life

Helpful and necessary, we hold it lightly

knowing that life is not so much about

finding the answers

but relishing the questions

Like a novice running around

clasping the recipe and shouting,

"these are the steps, this is the Way"

and coming into a Master Chef's house,

sees the banquet already laid out,

the chef taking delight in the smells, the tastes,

and the Joy of cooking and in awe,

the recipe silently falls from his fingertips

Unconditional...

I don't think any of us
can fathom unconditional love
the kind of total acceptance
that leaves nothing out.
We are so used to
judging ourselves harshly,
dividing ourselves up
into parts that are lovable
and parts that are not,
parts that we ostracize
and lock up,
never to be seen.
Unconditional love
is about union,
uniting and healing
the broken splinters
into wholeness,
like soaking in the deep, warm sunshine,

like soaking in the rays of the sun,
letting it warm each and every part,
until your whole being is bathed
in unconditional acceptance.
I don't think any of us
can fathom this kind of unconditional love,
this kind of freedom.
And what would the world be like
if we could accept this gift?
How would it change the way
we love others?
How would it change
the way we judge our neighbor?
Would there still be wars?
Could there still be enemies, hatred, and prejudice
or would this wholeness
also heal the brokenness
of our relationships
uniting us all
into the communion
from which we came.

The Illusion of Self

The self is not the solid thing
that we make it out to be,
but rather the capacity to experience
the reality of life,
to receive the beauty
and participate in her dance,
to share
in compassion and kindness,
to join in hands with one another
never giving in to the illusion
that the I is an entity.
For we are made to be permeable
Like the trees allow the wind
to blow through their branches.
Open

Identification with the self
is like having a body cast,
hard, closed off from the world, solid,
hidden from sight,
trapped beneath its walls,
lonely,
self-conscious,
dark,
afraid,
and loathsome.
But we are not made
to carry these illusions
as a reality,
but instead
to see beyond them
to transcend the borders
until they cease to exist.
This is how one loves another as himself.
This is how generosity is born,
forgiveness natural,
and hatred impossible.

Illusions

In the search for truth,

you must be willing to walk

through the dark forest of ignorance

with no light to guide you.

For it is only when the illusions

start to fall away

that you begin to see

the light of Awareness.

Wisdom of the Heart

The wisdom of the heart

speaks only in the silence.

She refuses to raise her voice

or compete with the noise

that threatens to drown her out.

Instead, she waits

for your arrival,

when you have stilled

your mind and heart

enough to hear

her gentle whispers

from within.

Pain

Sit with your pain,

draw it close,

be curious.

It will teach you more

when you embrace it

as a friend,

than when you resist it

like an enemy.

You will learn more

walking through its gates,

than years of sitting by the wayside,

denying it is there,

for it is in the embracing,

that wisdom comes.

The Puppet

The false self is like a puppet.

One can get caught up in the act,

yet all the while it's just a play,

a character,

a hallow shell.

All the while,

the truth,

is behind the veil.

Life as Kataphatic Prayer

God, I have to believe that you are present

in the cacophony of my daily life.

I cannot believe that the mystical life

is incompatible with the marketplace.

Although I protect my times of silent meditation

like a mother bear guards her cubs,

I know I live out the reality of my life with You

in the rest of my moving hours of the day.

I pray that the peace and depth I find in quiet

spills over into my interactions and relationships.

I pray that harmony resides

between my prayer and my life.

I hope that the transformation of stillness

floods into the activity of my day

like a rushing torrent.

I cannot barricade you out

or damn you up in my prayer closet.

No, you must be free to trickle into

every moment, thought, and word.

Yet, I must remember

to hold the patience of water too.

Like the long, slow process of erosion,

You change me slowly,

drip, drip, drip.

In my haste I cannot underestimate

the power of your grace.

Like water, in time, it can change

even the hardest of stone

and carve out vast spaces

for your Presence

to dwell in me always.

9 780099 133866 5